for sarah

love aunt debbie

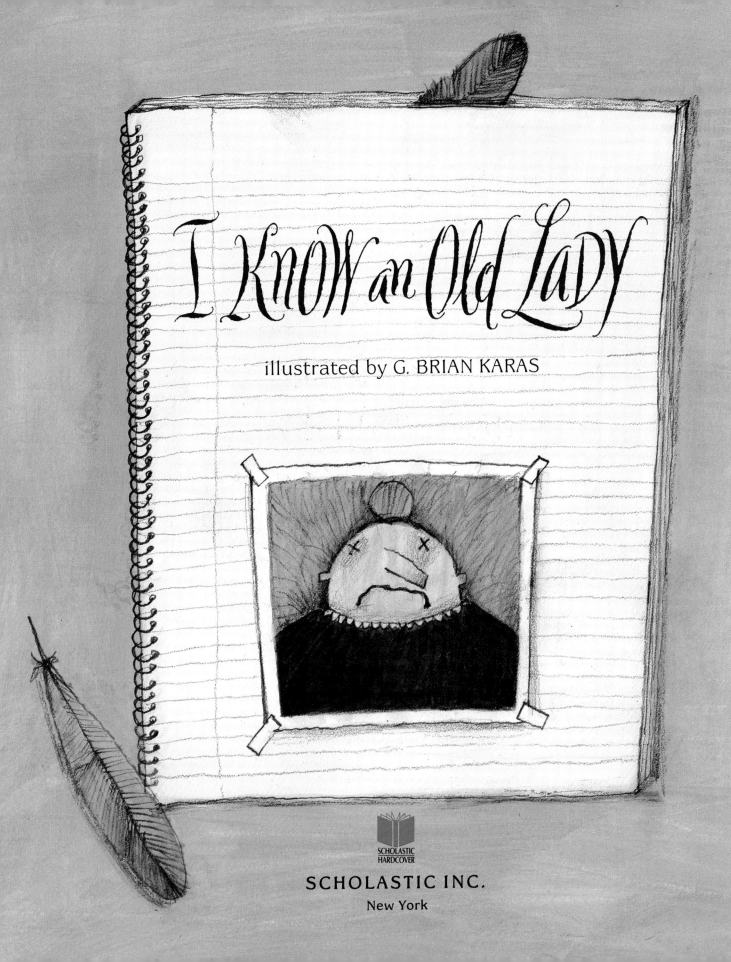

I Know an Old Lady

illustrated by G. BRIAN KARAS

SCHOLASTIC
HARDCOVER

SCHOLASTIC INC.

New York

Library of Congress Cataloging-in-Publication Data

Karas, G. Brian.
I know an old lady / by G. Brian Karas.
p.   cm.
Retelling of: Little old lady who swallowed a fly.
Summary: Retells the cumulative tale in which an old lady pays the
supreme penalty for her peculiar eating habits.
ISBN 0-590-46575-9
1.Folk songs, English — England — Texts. [1. Folk songs — England.
2. Nonsense verses.] I. Little old lady who swallowed a fly.
II. Title.
PZ8.3.K1264Iaf 1994
782.42162'21042 — dc20   93-30420
CIP
AC

12 11 10 9 8 7 6 5 4 3 2 1   4 5 6 7 8 9/9
Printed in the U.S.A.   37

Designed by Marijka Kostiw

The artist used gouache, acrylic, and pencil
for the illustrations in this book.

To Nicolette

I know an old lady who swallowed a fly. I don't know why she swallowed a fly. Perhaps she'll die.

I know an old lady who swallowed a spider

that wiggled and jiggled and tickled inside her.

She swallowed the spider to catch the fly. I don't know why she swallowed the fly. Perhaps she'll die.

I know an old lady who swallowed a bird. How absurd to swallow a bird.

She swallowed the bird to catch the spider that wiggled and jiggled and tickled inside her. She swallowed the spider to catch the fly. I don't know why she swallowed the fly. Perhaps she'll die.

I know an old lady who swallowed a cat. Imagine that, she swallowed a cat!

She swallowed the cat to catch the bird. She swallowed
the bird to catch the spider that wiggled and jiggled
and tickled inside her. She swallowed the spider to catch
the fly. I don't know why she swallowed the fly.
Perhaps she'll die.

I know an old lady who swallowed a dog. Oh, what a hog
to swallow a dog!

She swallowed the dog to catch the cat. She swallowed
the cat to catch the bird. She swallowed the bird to catch
the spider that wiggled and jiggled and tickled inside her.
She swallowed the spider to catch the fly. I don't know why
she swallowed the fly. Perhaps she'll die.

I know an old lady who swallowed a goat. Popped open
her throat to swallow a goat.

She swallowed the goat to catch the dog. She swallowed the dog to catch the cat. She swallowed the cat to catch the bird. She swallowed the bird to catch the spider that wiggled and jiggled and tickled inside her. She swallowed the spider to catch the fly. I don't know why she swallowed the fly. Perhaps she'll die.

I know an old lady who swallowed a cow. I don't know how
she swallowed a cow.

She swallowed the cow to catch the goat. She swallowed
the goat to catch the dog. She swallowed the dog to
catch the cat. She swallowed the cat to catch the bird.
She swallowed the bird to catch the spider that wiggled
and jiggled and tickled inside her. She swallowed the
spider to catch the fly. I don't know why she swallowed
the fly. Perhaps she'll die.

I know an old lady who swallowed a horse.

She died,

OF COURSE!